A Royal Ride

Catherine the Great's Great Invention

Kristen Fulton

ILLUSTRATED BY

Lucy Fleming

MARGARET K. McELDERRY BOOKS

New York London Toronto Sydney New Delhi

MARGARET K. McELDERRY BOOKS

An imprint of Simon & Schuster Children's Publishing Division

1230 Avenue of the Americas, New York, New York 10020

Text copyright © 2019 by Kristen Fulton

Illustrations copyright © 2019 by Lucy Fleming

MARGARET K. McELDERRY BOOKS is a trademark of Simon & Schuster, Inc. · For information about special discounts for bulk purchases, please contact Simon & Schuster Special Sales at 1-866-506-1949 or business@simonandschuster.com. · The Simon & Schuster Speakers Bureau can bring authors to your live event. For more information or to book an event, contact the Simon & Schuster Speakers Bureau at 1-866-248-3049 or visit our website at www.simonspeakers.com. · Book design by Debra Sfetsios-Conover · The text for this book was set in Alghera Std. · The illustrations for this book were rendered in Adobe Photoshop CC 2018. · Manufactured in China · 0419 SCP · First Edition · 10 9 8 7 6 5 4 3 2 1

Library of Congress Cataloging-in-Publication Data

Names: Fulton, Kristen. · Title: A royal ride : Catherine the Great's great invention / Kristen Fulton ; illustrated by Lucy Fleming. · Description: New York : Margaret K. McElderry Books, An imprint of Simon & Schuster Children's Publishing Division, 2019. · Identifiers: LCCN 2018013328 (print) | ISBN 9781481496575 (hardcover) | ISBN 9781481496582 (eBook) · Subjects: LCSH: Catherine II, Empress of Russia, 1729–1796—Juvenile literature. | Roller coasters—Juvenile literature. · Classification: LCC DK170.F85 2019 (print) | DDC 947/.063092 [B]—dc23 · LC record available at https://lccn.loc.gov/2018013328

To Marie. Thank you for being up for the adventure and going to Russia with me.
—K. F.

For Lincoln
—L. F.

CATHERINE THE GREAT, Empress of Russia, wasn't born in Russia.

But she loved everything about the country.

Catherine believed that everyone should be educated, not just boys or the wealthy.

She formed the first school for girls in Russia and she sponsored the University of Moscow.

Learning about art, culture, and the history of Russia was important to all the citizens. So Catherine directed the building of the Hermitage Museum.

But when winter came, Catherine's mind
sometimes wandered.

Snowflakes falling, temperatures dropping,
and the icy mantle that covered the land—
she loved it all.

She found it hard to concentrate . . .

because the beginning of winter meant
ICE SLIDES!

People lined the streets of Saint Petersburg
waiting for the royal sign.

A wave of Catherine's hand would declare
ice slide season officially open.

This Way

In her jeweled tiara and tapestry gown, Catherine rushed to her own private slide. She climbed the steep ladder and nestled onto her sled. With the reins held tight, she bolted, barreled, and breezed six hundred feet down a solid sheet of ice.

But every spring the fun came to an end.
The sun shone so bright and hot that it melted
the snow and ice, washing the slides away.
There were no more daring descents or
thrilling rides.

For the next six months the queen wondered
what would she do.

Build a hospital?

Open a theater?

Write her memoirs?

Catherine wanted more.

She called her royal builders and made a most royal request.

The builders had built schools, palaces, and museums under Catherine's order.

But now she wanted them to build a new kind of slide.

She wanted to sail through the air and she didn't want to wait until winter.

There had to be a way to soar in the sun.

Grabbing parchment and quill, Catherine drew
what she had imagined.

Gilded beams
and poles as high as
a mountain.
Golden stairs
that spiraled all the
way to the top.
With one last
flourish, Catherine's
design was complete.

Giving the sketch to the builders, she ordered
them to work.

Day after day, the royal gardens filled with supplies and tools.

From the palace, Catherine glanced, gazed, then glared.

WOOD?

The builders couldn't use wood; there must be a mistake.

Where was the gold she had envisioned? Where were the diamonds and the rubies befitting an empress?

If she slid on wood, her royal bum would be filled with splinters and aches.

Summoning the builders, she questioned each one.

Everyone agreed that the queen's idea was ingenious.

But gold was too soft. They had to use wood.

They promised the empress that her safety and comfort were their number one concerns.

The builders returned to work.

As Catherine awaited her royal ride, there was still so much to do. She had a country to rule. She sent her army off to war. She purchased statues. She moved into a new castle. And she even wrote a book.

But the builders still weren't done.

Finally, one late summer day, her royal ride was ready.

With her ladies-in-waiting trailing behind, Catherine rushed to the gardens.

She was the first in line.

She climbed forty feet in the air.
Catherine stopped to catch her breath.
Then she climbed to the top amidst all
the stares.

At the top Catherine stared at her fandangled carriage. The gems glittered just for her. She was the empress, after all.

Catherine took a deep breath, leaped in, and was ready to whirl.

With a shove, and the whoosh of the wind,
Catherine plunged, plummeted, and plowed to
the bottom.

She rolled and coasted to the end of the track.

Her daring descent.

The thrill of her ride.

Catherine had no idea that her man-made
Russian mountain was the world's first roller
coaster.

But Empress Catherine the Great, ruler of Russia, knew one thing for sure:

GO!
GO!
GO!

She was ready to go again.

And AGAIN!

And AGAIN!

AUTHOR'S NOTE

Yes, Catherine the Great is credited for the invention of the roller coaster. But it took over a hundred years before it evolved into what we know today as the loop-the-loop, speeding, plunging roller coaster. Through the years, engineers have tweaked, added, and improved on Catherine's original idea. A French engineer added a pulley system that would hoist each carriage back up to the top. A British engineer added a loop, but the cart had to be going very fast or it would drop in the middle of the loop. Finally, an American engineer, LaMarcus Adna Thompson, received a patent for the roller coaster and added a motor that kept the cart powered through the entire ride.

In many languages today, the word "roller coaster" is translated as "Russian mountains."

French: montagnes russes
Romanian: montagnes russes
Italian: montagne russe
Portuguese: montanha russa
Spanish: montaña rusa
Icelandic: rússíbani
Basque: errusiar mendi
Catalan: muntanya russa
Corsican: muntagna russa
Danish: rutsjebane
Galician: montaña rusa
Czech: horská dráha

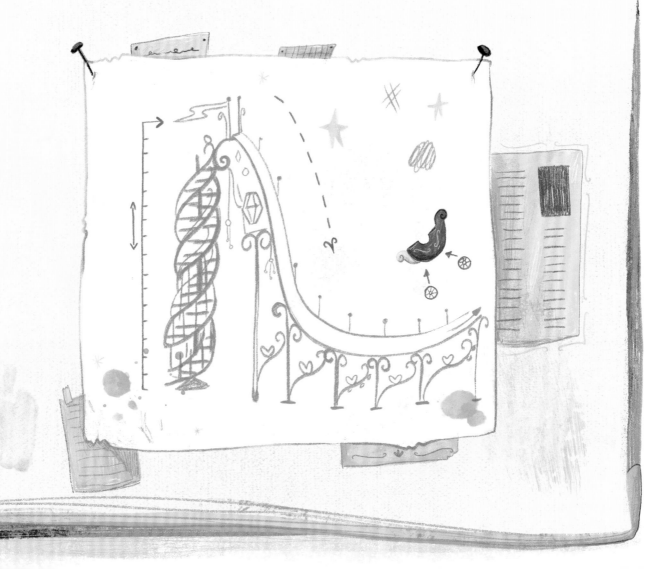

ICE SLIDES

~1400~

ROLLER COASTER TIME LINE:

1400s The first Russian ice slides appear, only used during winter.

1784 Catherine the Great unveils her summer slide that uses a rail system to operate all year long.

1817 The first rides designed with wheels and pulley systems are built in Paris.

1840 The world's first looping roller coaster is designed and built in Britain.

1873 The Mauch Chunk Railway in Pennsylvania becomes the first ride to form a complete circuit.

1817

PARIS

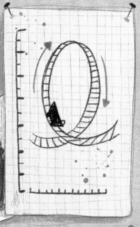

1891 The first coaster with a vertical loop is built and opens.

1907 Drop-the-Dips roller coaster opens and is the first to use a lap-bar style restraint.

1979 The world's longest roller coaster, The Beast (7,359 feet), opens at Kings Island in Cincinnati, OH. It is still the world's longest wooden roller coaster.

THE BEAST

1980 The first roller coaster to have four inversions opens at Carowinds in Charlotte, NC.

1982 Viper at Darien Lake in Darien Center, NY, opens. It is the world's first roller coaster to feature five inversions.

VIPER
~1982~

1982 The world's first stand-up roller coaster opens in Japan.

BIBLIOGRAPHY:

Alexander, John T. *Catherine the Great: Life and Legend*. New York: Oxford University Press, 1989.

Massie, Suzanne. *Land of the Firebird: The Beauty of Old Russia*. New York: Simon & Schuster, 1980.

"Modest Ice Slide Started Coaster Craze That's Still Rolling." *Daily Herald* (Arlington Heights, IL), July 11, 2001. Accessed June 8, 2015.

Oldenbourg, Zoé. *Catherine the Great*. New York: Pantheon, 1965.

Royal archives. Russian State Library, Moscow.

Sandy, Adam. "The Beginning." "Roller Coaster History: How It Started." UltimateRollercoaster.com. Accessed July 9, 2015. https://www.ultimaterollercoaster.com/coasters/history/start/

ACKNOWLEDGMENTS

A very special thank-you to the Russian State Library in Moscow and to the American Center Library at the U.S. Embassy in Moscow for helping me gather my research while visiting this historical city.

OPENING SOON!

TAGE
EUM